anything

Claymation Sensation

# UNDERWATER CLAYMATION

Emily Reid

WINDMILL
BOOKS

Published in 2017 by **Windmill Books**,
an Imprint of Rosen Publishing
29 East 21st Street, New York, NY 10010

Produced for Rosen by BlueAppleWorks Inc.

Creative Director: Melissa McClellan
Managing Editor for BlueAppleWorks: Melissa McClellan
Design: T.J. Choleva
Editor: Kelly Spence
Puppet Artisans: Janet Kompare-Fritz (p. 20); Sandor Monos (p. 14, 22); Jane Yates (p. 10, 12, 16, 18)

Picture credits: Plasticine letters: Vitaly Korovin/Shutterstock; title page, TOC, Austen Photography; p. 4 Lionsgate/Photofest;
p.5 Janet Kompare-Fritz; p. 6 left to right and top to bottom: ukrfidget/Shutterstock; Andrey Eremin/Shutterstock; exopixel
/Shutterstock; Lukas Gojda/Shutterstock; koosen/Shutterstock; Irina Nartova/Shutterstock; STILLFX/Shutterstock; Darryl
Brooks/Shutterstock; Winai Tepsuttinun/Shutterstock; Yulia elf_inc Tropina/Shutterstock; Austen Photography; All For
You /Shutterstock; AlenKadr/Shutterstock; Radu Bercan /Shutterstock; Austen Photography; p. 7 left to right and top to
bottom: Ilike/Shutterstock; Tarzhanova/Shutterstock; Austen Photography; kamomeen /Shutterstock; Lesha/Shutterstock;
ikurdyumov/Shutterstock; Austen Photography; Ilike/Shutterstock; p-8 to 27 Austen Photography; p. 28 left Valentina
Razumova/Shutterstock; p. 29 upper left Warongdech/Shutterstock;p. 29 top right Anneka/Shutterstock; p. 29 right taelove7/
Shutterstock; p. 30, 31 Austen Photography

Cataloging-in-Publication Data
Names: Reid, Emily.
Title: Underwater claymation / Emily Reid.
Description: New York : Windmill Books, 2017. | Series: Claymation sensation | Includes index.
Identifiers: ISBN 9781499481082 (pbk.) | ISBN 9781499481105 (library bound) | ISBN 9781499481099 (6 pack)
Subjects: LCSH: Animation (Cinematography)--Juvenile literature. | Sculpture--Technique--Juvenile literature. | Sea in art--
    Juvenile literature.
Classification: LCC TR897.5 R45 2017 | DDC 777'.7--dc23

Manufactured in the United States of America
CPSIA Compliance Information: Batch #BS16PK: For Further Information contact Rosen Publishing, New York, New York at 1-800-237-9932

# Contents

# What Is Claymation?

Are you ready to dive into the exciting world of Claymation? Claymation, also known as clay **animation**, combines **stop-motion** animation with characters or puppets made out of modeling clay to create movies or short videos.

Stop-motion animation creates the illusion of movement when a series of still images, called **frames**, are quickly played in sequence. Each frame shows a slight change in position from the previous frame. Clay characters are easy to move and reposition to show these actions in small steps. The smaller the movements, the smoother the sequence appears. It takes several frames to make a Claymation movie. Animations can be created using many devices, including a traditional camera, smartphone, or tablet.

*Full-length Claymation movies and TV shows take months and lots of money to make.* The Shaun the Sheep Movie, *released in 2015, took twenty animators and ten months to produce.*

## Claymation Tip

*There are lots of apps you can use to create your Claymation movie. These apps let you shoot and edit your movie using one device. Make sure to ask permission before you download any apps to your smartphone, tablet, or computer.*

All types of filmmaking, including Claymation, tell a story. To start, brainstorm an idea for your underwater adventure. Think of a beginning, middle, and end. Write a short summary of the story. How many characters do you need to tell your story? What kind of background and props will you use?

When you make a Claymation movie, it is important to map out the character's movements before you start shooting. A **storyboard** is a series of drawings that show each step of the story. Use a storyboard to figure out what actions are needed, and in what order, to tell your story from start to finish. Sketch out each scene and label it with the scene number. After the storyboard is ready, it's time to create your puppets.

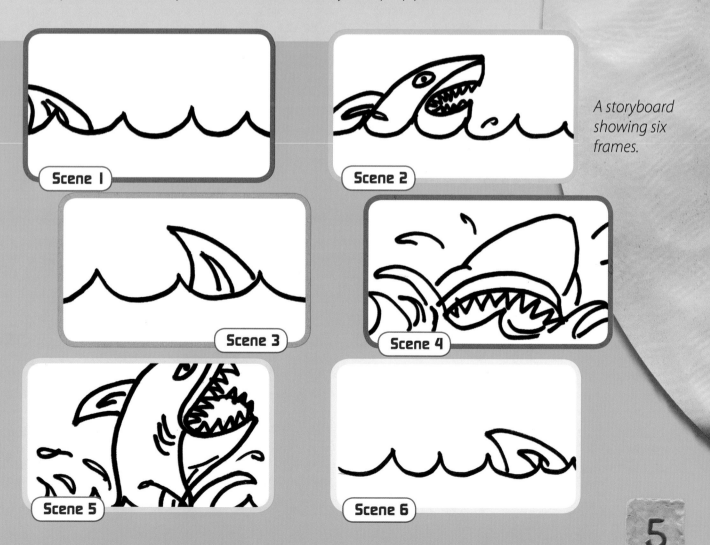

*A storyboard showing six frames.*

Scene 1

Scene 2

Scene 3

Scene 4

Scene 5

Scene 6

# Materials and Techniques

Claymation puppets are created with nondrying, oil-based clay. Plasticine is a popular brand, although any nondrying modeling clay will do. This type of clay is moldable enough to create a character, flexible enough to allow that character to move in many ways, and dense enough to hold its shape when combined with a wire **armature**.

## Materials That You Will Need

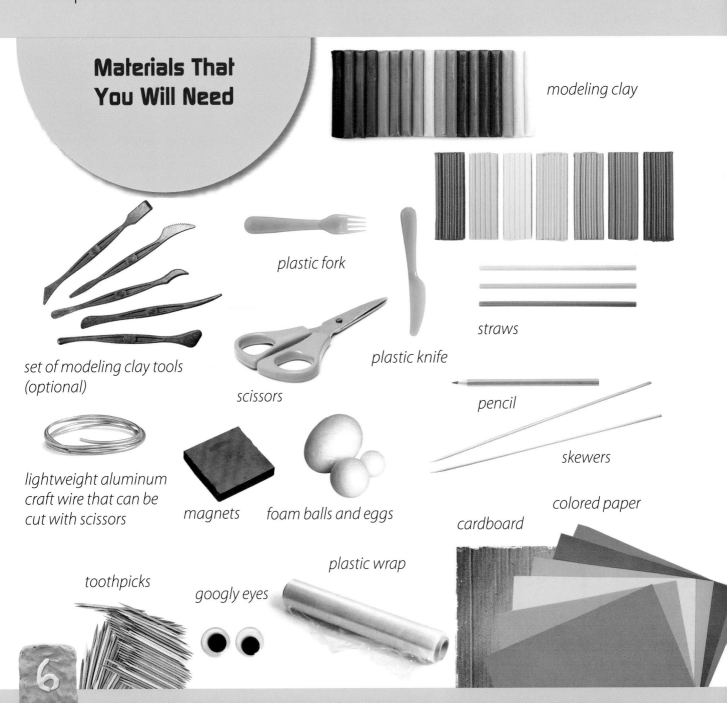

modeling clay

set of modeling clay tools (optional)

plastic fork

plastic knife

straws

scissors

pencil

skewers

lightweight aluminum craft wire that can be cut with scissors

magnets

foam balls and eggs

cardboard

colored paper

toothpicks

googly eyes

plastic wrap

## Working with Clay

Modeling clay is oily and can be messy to work with. Prepare a work area. A piece of cardboard or foam board is great to work on. Wash your hands well when you finish working, as they will be oily, too.

## Basic Shapes

All of these shapes can be made big or small or thin or thick, depending on the amount of clay used and the pressure applied. Use your fingers to squish, smooth, pinch, flatten, and poke the clay into whatever shape you want.

*To form a ball, move your hands in a circle while pressing the clay lightly between them.*

*To create a pancake shape, roll a ball and flatten it between your thumb and fingers. Smooth the edges if they crack.*

*To make a snake shape, roll the clay on a flat surface with your fingers.*

*To form a teardrop, pinch and roll one end of a ball into a point.*

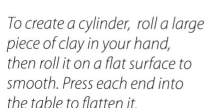

*To create a cylinder, roll a large piece of clay in your hand, then roll it on a flat surface to smooth. Press each end into the table to flatten it.*

*To make a slab, start with a large piece and flatten it on your work surface. Keep pressing the clay out and away from the center until it is as flat as you want it.*

## Modeling Tips

● Always start by kneading the clay in your hands to warm it up and soften it.

● You can mix different colors together to create new colors. Just squish the clay in your hands until it is blended completely or leave it partially blended to create a marble effect.

● Make your puppets about the same size as an action figure, between 4 and 6 inches (10 and 15 cm) tall. They should be big enough to move around but not so big they fall over.

# Body Parts and Armatures

Puppets can be made in many ways. The simple ones require only modeling clay and some patience. If you decide to create more complicated puppets, you will need additional elements to give the puppets structure and support, such as wire armatures and foam shapes. It is a good idea to keep anything that is on top of the puppet light so it does not droop during animation. Using a lightweight foam ball should do the trick.

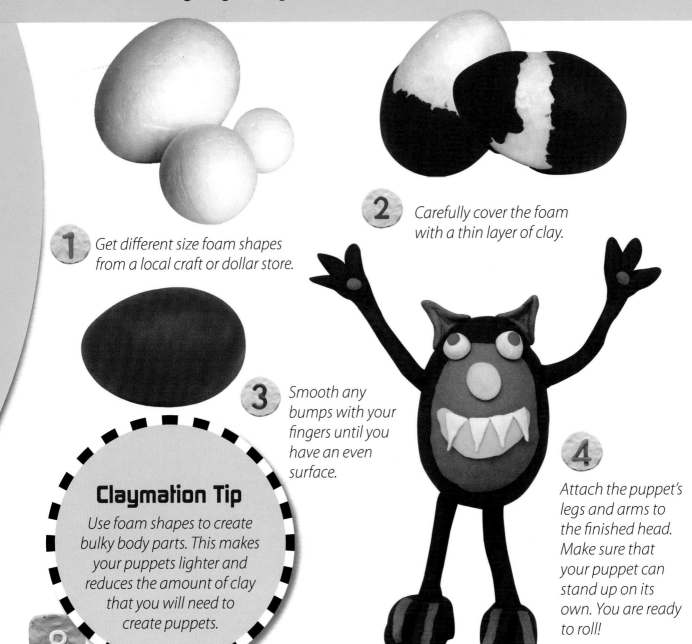

**1** Get different size foam shapes from a local craft or dollar store.

**2** Carefully cover the foam with a thin layer of clay.

**3** Smooth any bumps with your fingers until you have an even surface.

**4** Attach the puppet's legs and arms to the finished head. Make sure that your puppet can stand up on its own. You are ready to roll!

### Claymation Tip

Use foam shapes to create bulky body parts. This makes your puppets lighter and reduces the amount of clay that you will need to create puppets.

## Stability

Make sure your character has a big enough base or feet to support its weight. If necessary, you can stabilize it with putty or put pushpins through the puppet's feet to hold it in place.

## Armatures

Armatures function as a skeleton that holds the puppet parts together and allows for them to move easily. Wire-based armatures are made using strands of lightweight wire. Whenever useful, you can combine an armature with foam pieces to create a base for your puppet. Make sure you don't make the clay too thick around the armature, or your puppet will be difficult to move.

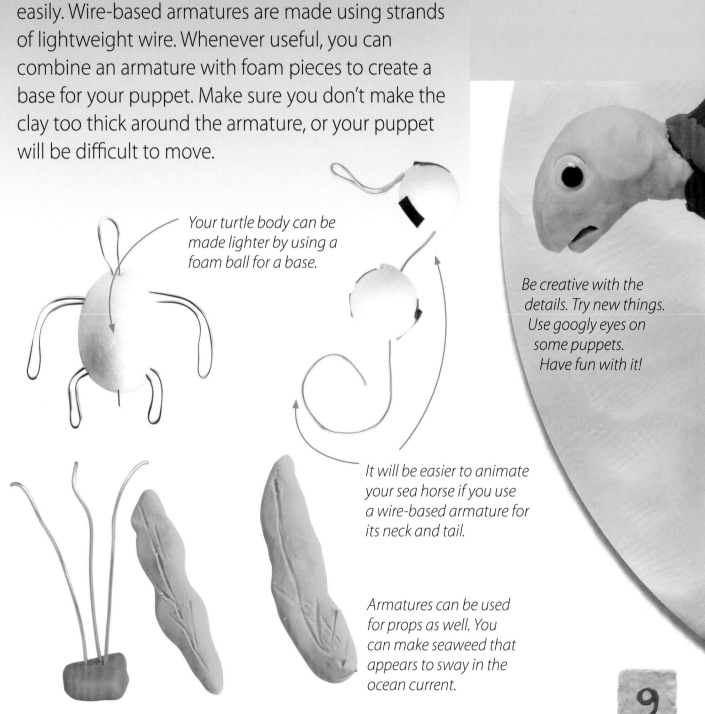

*Your turtle body can be made lighter by using a foam ball for a base.*

*Be creative with the details. Try new things. Use googly eyes on some puppets. Have fun with it!*

*It will be easier to animate your sea horse if you use a wire-based armature for its neck and tail.*

*Armatures can be used for props as well. You can make seaweed that appears to sway in the ocean current.*

9

# Shark Puppet

Great white sharks are one of the largest predators in the sea. A great white can smell blood up to 3 miles (5 km) away. These giant fish are mostly bluish-gray, with a bright white belly. Their mouths are lined with several rows of sharp teeth.

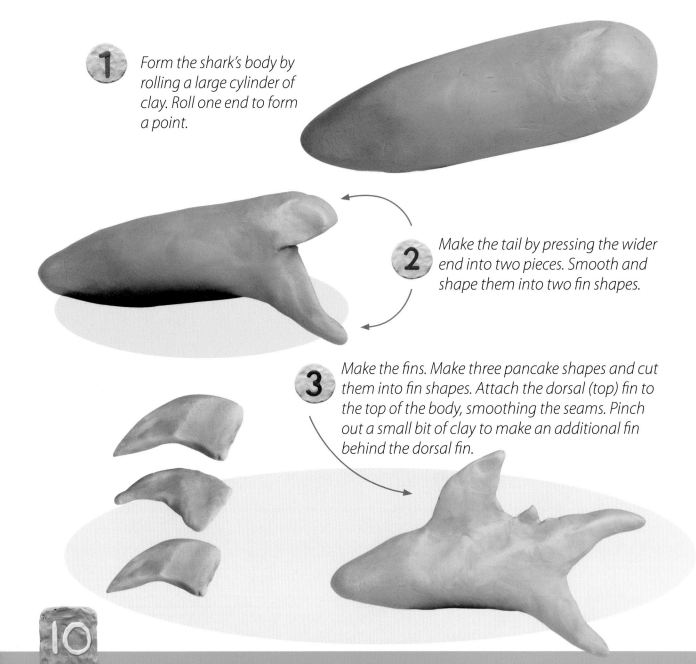

**1** *Form the shark's body by rolling a large cylinder of clay. Roll one end to form a point.*

**2** *Make the tail by pressing the wider end into two pieces. Smooth and shape them into two fin shapes.*

**3** *Make the fins. Make three pancake shapes and cut them into fin shapes. Attach the dorsal (top) fin to the top of the body, smoothing the seams. Pinch out a small bit of clay to make an additional fin behind the dorsal fin.*

**4** Make the belly by smoothing white clay over the bottom of the shark's body. Smooth the edges.

**5** For the gills, make slits in the side of the shark's head using a skewer.

**6** Make a flat rectangle of white clay. Cut out triangles to form teeth. Press this onto the top and bottom of the mouth and blend. Make a pink oval, flatten it, and insert it in the mouth for a tongue.

**7** Press the two fins made in Step 3 into the sides of the shark. Smooth the edges.

**8** For the eyes, press a small ball into each side of the head.

### Claymation Tip

When animating your puppet, attach the shark to a toothpick or stick with a lump of clay on the other end. The shark can be moved around and the stick will be hidden behind the water. To create a suspenseful scene, hide the shark behind the water with only the dorsal fin showing, then turn it so the whole shark and its sharp white teeth are visible.

# Fish Puppet

Tropical fish are very colorful and can be found in the warm waters of the Indian and Pacific Oceans. They live at the bottom of the sea in sheltered reefs or in shallow lagoons.

**1** *Use a lightweight foam ball for the body to make the puppet lighter. Use a thin piece of cardboard to make two fins and tail. To attach the fins and tail, carefully cut small slots into the fish's body with a butter knife. Stick the cardboard into the slits.*

**2** *Carefully cover the body with a thin layer of clay.*

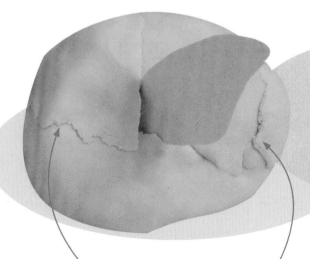

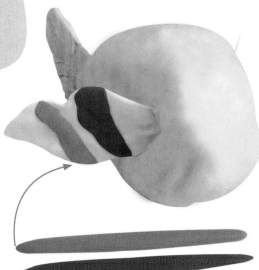

**3** *Smooth the edges together using your fingers.*

**4** *Cover the fins and tail with clay. Make two narrow rolls and flatten them on the fin to create stripes. Repeat this step for the other fin. Make blue stripes and add them to the tail.*

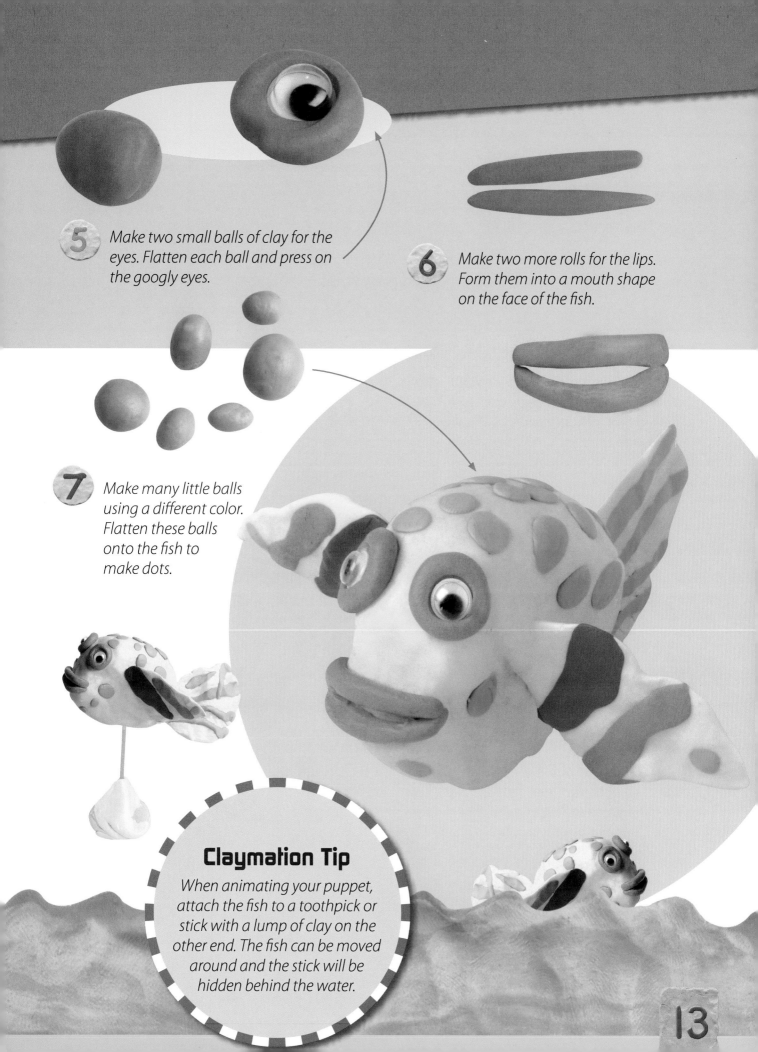

**5** Make two small balls of clay for the eyes. Flatten each ball and press on the googly eyes.

**6** Make two more rolls for the lips. Form them into a mouth shape on the face of the fish.

**7** Make many little balls using a different color. Flatten these balls onto the fish to make dots.

## Claymation Tip

*When animating your puppet, attach the fish to a toothpick or stick with a lump of clay on the other end. The fish can be moved around and the stick will be hidden behind the water.*

# Turtle Puppet

Sea turtles are sometimes called marine turtles. They are some of the oldest animals on Earth. Sea turtles swim along the ocean floor, feeding on sea grasses, shrimp, snails, and other small creatures.

**1** Make an armature for the puppet with an egg-shaped piece of foam and five pieces of wire. Bend each piece of wire in half and insert it into the body as shown.

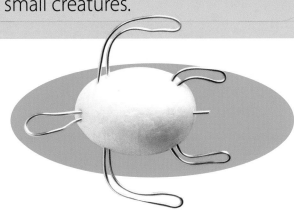

**2** Make a thick pancake shape for the head and fold it over the wire. Make four smaller pancake shapes for the legs. Place each piece over the wire and shape it into a fin.

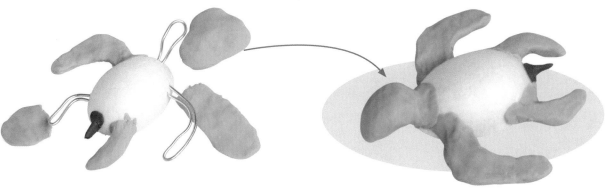

**3** Make a thin slab of clay. Completely cover the body and tail with the slab. Smooth the edges.

**4** Make a thin pancake of clay and press it onto the bottom of the turtle.

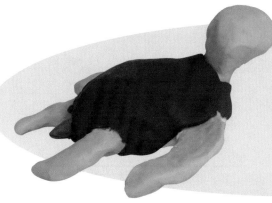
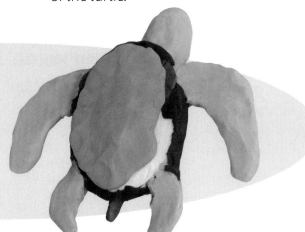

14

**5** Make a thick roll and place it around the top to form the shell. Pinch it to make a scalloped edge.

**7** Use the modeling tool to make the mouth. Press two googly eyes into the head.

**6** Use the modeling tool to make indentations across the top of the shell.

**8** Make several little balls and press them into the turtle's fins and head to create dots.

**9** Roll out five snake shapes and press them into the indentations.

### Claymation Tip

When animating your turtle puppet, it can move along the ocean floor looking for something tasty to eat. The armature flippers will be easy to move.

# Sea Lion Puppet

A sea lion lives on the shore but is able to dive underwater to catch fish. These loud animals can stay underwater for nearly ten minutes at a time. Sea lions live together in large colonies.

**1** Start with a large piece of clay. Roll it into an oval shape. One end should be a bit narrower than the other. Set some extra clay aside for the front fins.

**2** Bend the narrow end up and forward in an S shape to make the neck and head of the sea lion.

**3** Use a modeling tool to split the end of the body into two. Pinch each of these ends into flippers and pull them to the side of the sea lion.

**4** Form two flipper-shaped pieces and press them into the front sides of the sea lion.

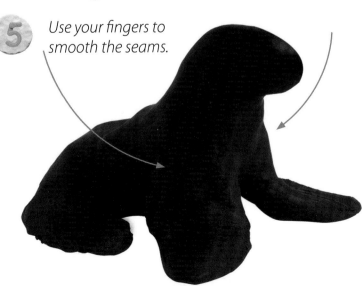

**5** Use your fingers to smooth the seams.

16

**6** Use a modeling tool to make indentations in all four flippers. Then use the tool to make the mouth.

**7** Make two tiny half-circle shapes for ears and press one onto each side of the head.

**8** Make a small triangle out of clay and press it onto the end of the sea lion's nose. Flatten two white balls. Place two flattened blue balls on top and press into the head for eyes.

**9** Roll several little balls. Flatten these balls onto the sea lion to make dots.

**Claymation Tip**

When animating your sea lion puppet, it can move along or it can be bent to sit on its back flippers.

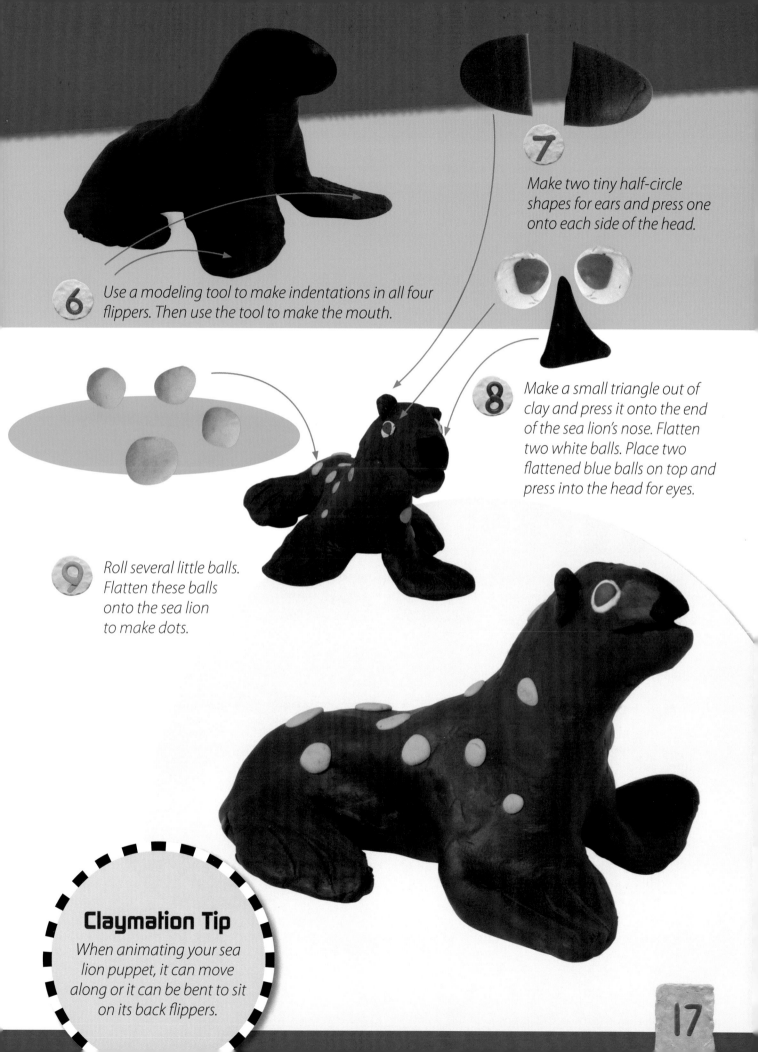

# Octopus Puppet

Octopuses have eight arms that are covered in suckers. These animals usually live on the ocean floor. They move very quickly and are great at hiding. When octopuses swim, their arms trail behind them.

**1** *Start with two sets of eight small rolls of clay in two different colors.*

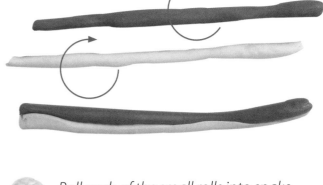

**2** *Roll each of the small rolls into snake shapes. Press one roll of each color together to form a two-sided arm.*

**3** *Repeat Step 2 until you have eight arms.*

**4** *Make a small pancake shape for the head. Place a small foam ball in the middle.*

**5** Wrap the clay around the ball, smoothing it down. Form a base with the extra clay.

**6** Turn the head upside down. Press the ends of the arms into the base clay. Smooth the edge of the base and tentacles together.

**7** Use the modeling tool to make a hole for the mouth. Flatten two white ovals, add two flattened blue balls on top, then press into the head for eyes.

**8** Make several tiny balls using a different color clay. Flatten these balls onto the bottom of the arms to make suckers. Press some snake shapes onto the head.

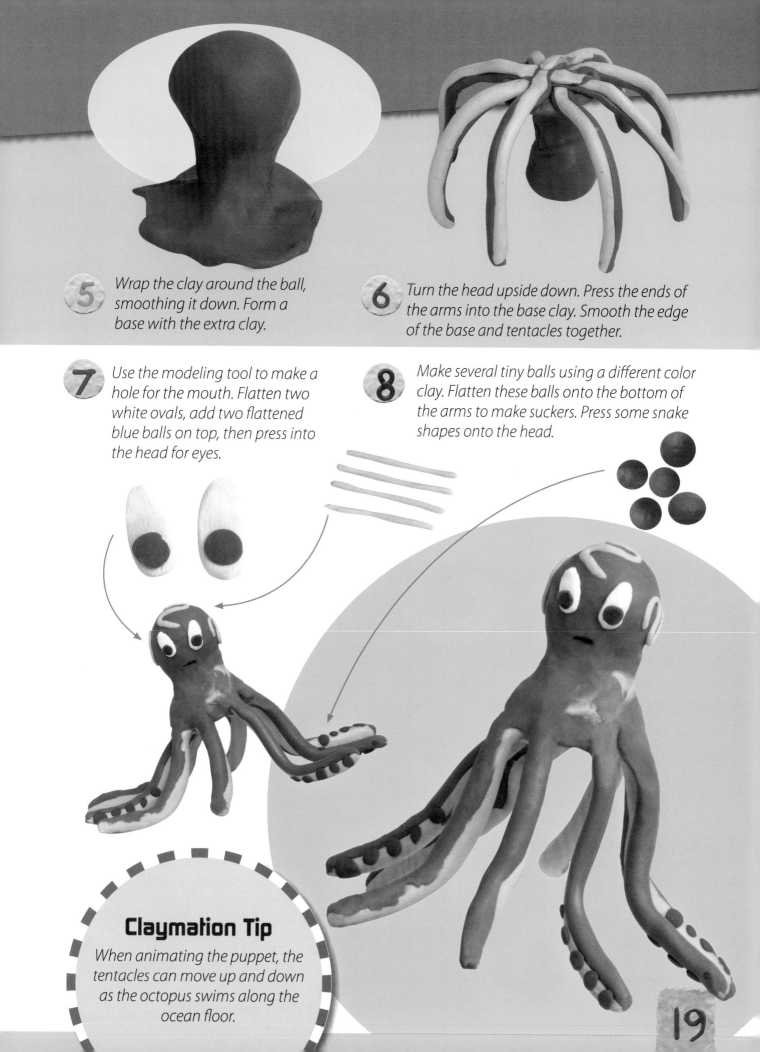

### Claymation Tip
*When animating the puppet, the tentacles can move up and down as the octopus swims along the ocean floor.*

19

# Sea Horse Puppet

Sea horses are beautiful marine fish that resemble horses with their long snout. They have flexible necks and are poor swimmers. To stay in one spot, sea horses use their long, curled tails to anchor to coral and sea grasses growing on the ocean floor.

**1** Carefully cut a foam ball in half. Bend a piece of craft wire into the shape of the sea horse. Tape it to the back of the two halves of the ball to create your armature.

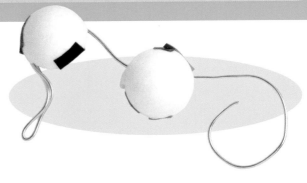

**2** Carefully cover the armature with a thin layer of clay in different colors. Smooth the edges together using your fingers.

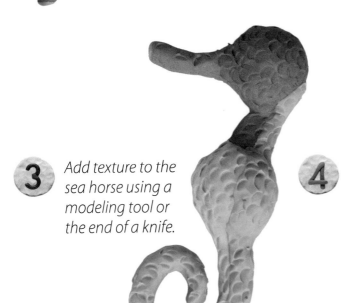

**3** Add texture to the sea horse using a modeling tool or the end of a knife.

**4** Roll out long snake shapes in a contrasting color. Make a crisscross pattern, covering the sea horse's body and tail.

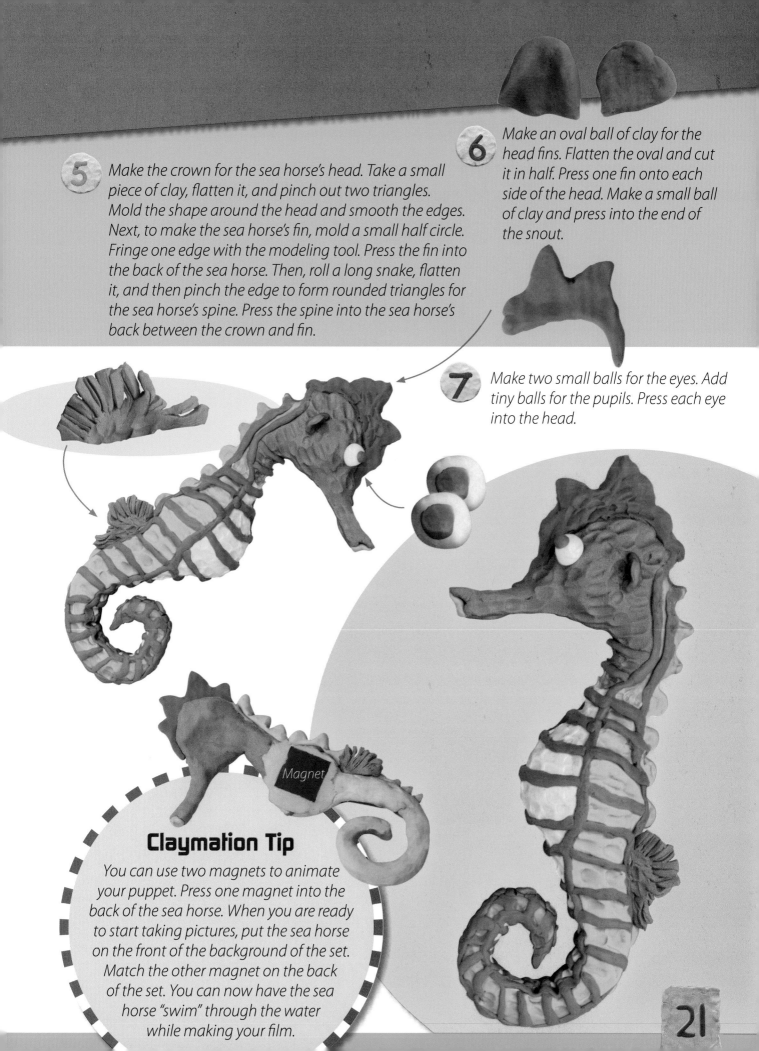

**5** Make the crown for the sea horse's head. Take a small piece of clay, flatten it, and pinch out two triangles. Mold the shape around the head and smooth the edges. Next, to make the sea horse's fin, mold a small half circle. Fringe one edge with the modeling tool. Press the fin into the back of the sea horse. Then, roll a long snake, flatten it, and then pinch the edge to form rounded triangles for the sea horse's spine. Press the spine into the sea horse's back between the crown and fin.

**6** Make an oval ball of clay for the head fins. Flatten the oval and cut it in half. Press one fin onto each side of the head. Make a small ball of clay and press into the end of the snout.

**7** Make two small balls for the eyes. Add tiny balls for the pupils. Press each eye into the head.

## Claymation Tip

You can use two magnets to animate your puppet. Press one magnet into the back of the sea horse. When you are ready to start taking pictures, put the sea horse on the front of the background of the set. Match the other magnet on the back of the set. You can now have the sea horse "swim" through the water while making your film.

Magnet

# Stingray Puppet

Stingrays are found on the bottom of the sea near the shoreline. Their bodies are wide and flat. They swim along the ocean floor by moving their body like a wave. Stingrays use their long, spiky tails to keep enemies away. Some species have a poisonous sting.

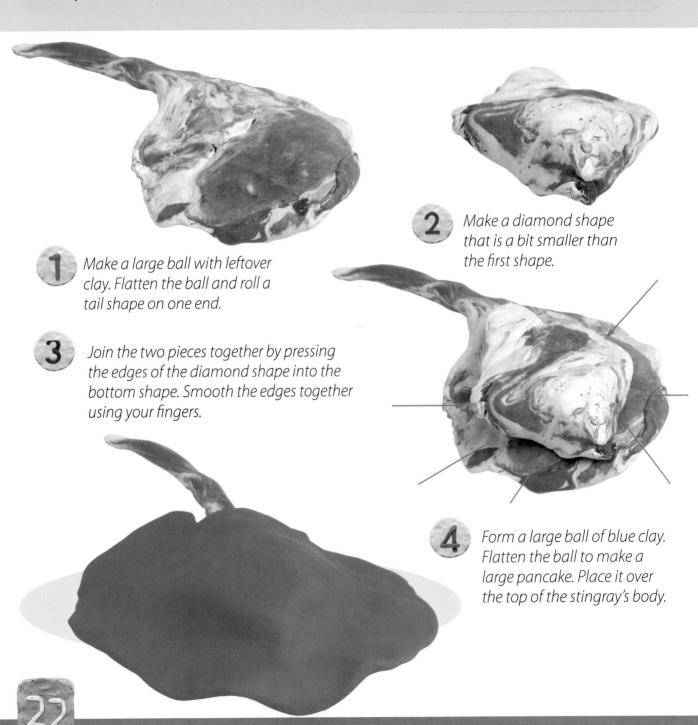

1 Make a large ball with leftover clay. Flatten the ball and roll a tail shape on one end.

2 Make a diamond shape that is a bit smaller than the first shape.

3 Join the two pieces together by pressing the edges of the diamond shape into the bottom shape. Smooth the edges together using your fingers.

4 Form a large ball of blue clay. Flatten the ball to make a large pancake. Place it over the top of the stingray's body.

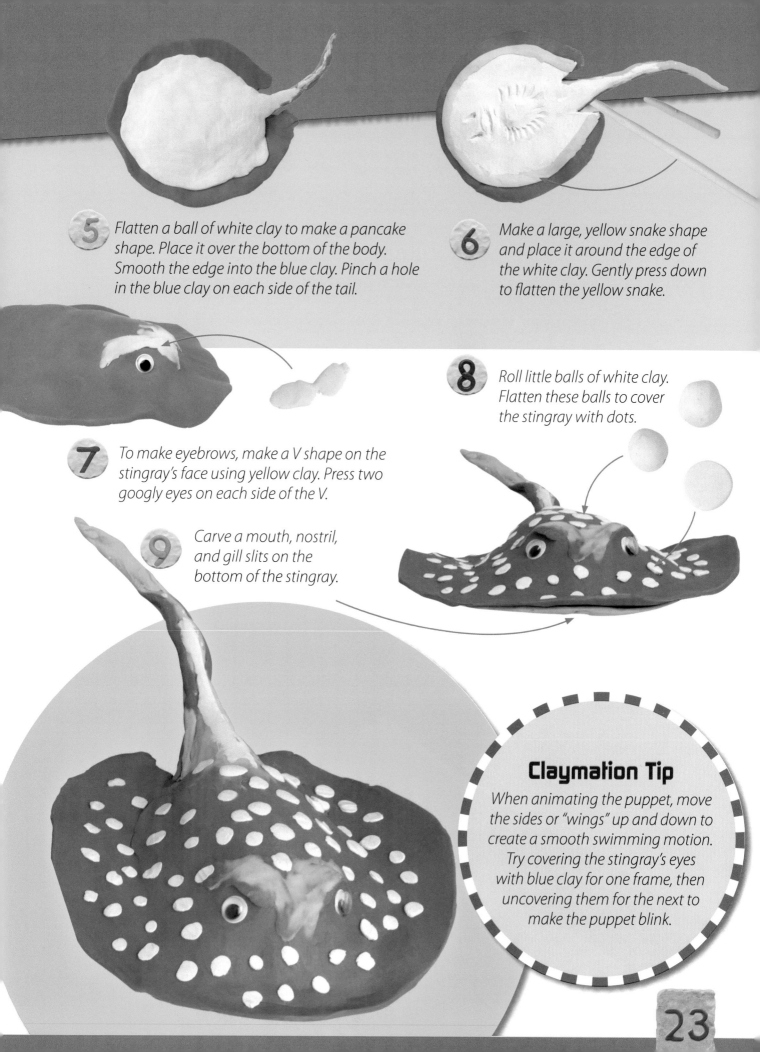

**5** Flatten a ball of white clay to make a pancake shape. Place it over the bottom of the body. Smooth the edge into the blue clay. Pinch a hole in the blue clay on each side of the tail.

**6** Make a large, yellow snake shape and place it around the edge of the white clay. Gently press down to flatten the yellow snake.

**8** Roll little balls of white clay. Flatten these balls to cover the stingray with dots.

**7** To make eyebrows, make a V shape on the stingray's face using yellow clay. Press two googly eyes on each side of the V.

**9** Carve a mouth, nostril, and gill slits on the bottom of the stingray.

### Claymation Tip

When animating the puppet, move the sides or "wings" up and down to create a smooth swimming motion. Try covering the stingray's eyes with blue clay for one frame, then uncovering them for the next to make the puppet blink.

# The Props

Props are used in movies to decorate the set. In an underwater film the props can be anything you would find on the bottom of the sea. Props add visual interest to the movie. Sometimes the puppets interact with them.

**2** *Make seaweed by making a small, flat pancake shape. Pinch out four or five fingers. Use a modeling tool to add extra details. Press down to flatten the bottom, or make a bottom from another color and press them together.*

**1** *Make coral by rolling small snake shapes in different colors. Add texture with a modeling tool. Cluster four or five pieces together. Press the ends together to form a small coral reef.*

**3** *Make rocks by combining several dark colors of clay. Squish them together, but not so much that the colors become blended. Press your thumb into the ball three or four times in different spots to make the rocks bumpy.*

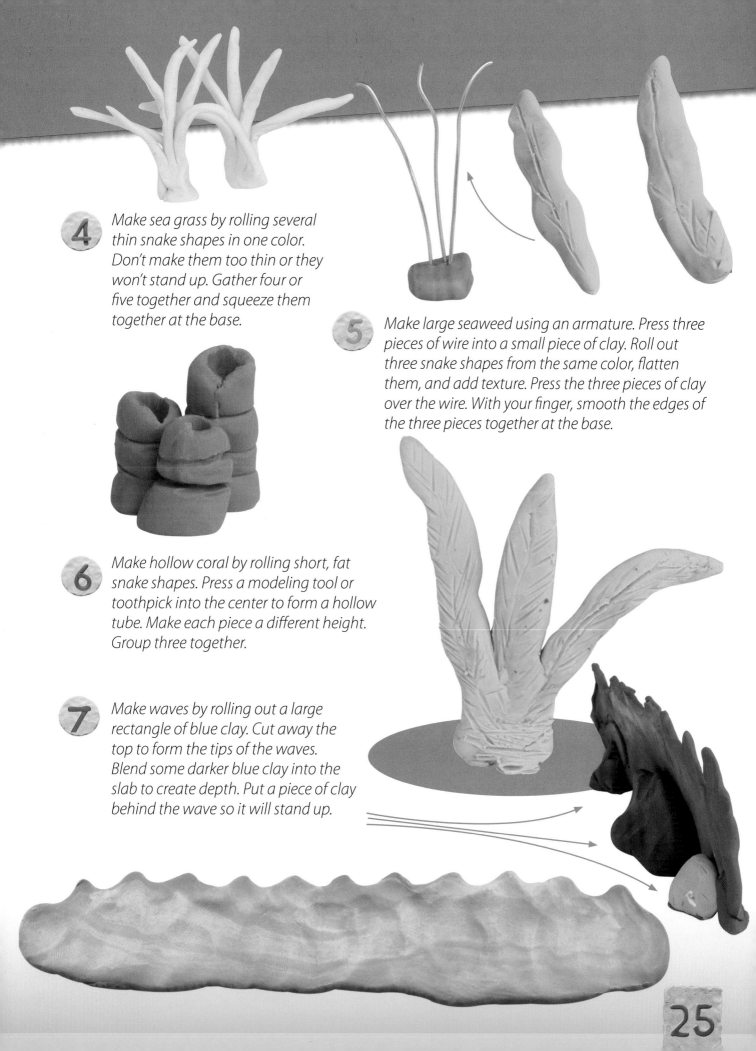

**4** Make sea grass by rolling several thin snake shapes in one color. Don't make them too thin or they won't stand up. Gather four or five together and squeeze them together at the base.

**5** Make large seaweed using an armature. Press three pieces of wire into a small piece of clay. Roll out three snake shapes from the same color, flatten them, and add texture. Press the three pieces of clay over the wire. With your finger, smooth the edges of the three pieces together at the base.

**6** Make hollow coral by rolling short, fat snake shapes. Press a modeling tool or toothpick into the center to form a hollow tube. Make each piece a different height. Group three together.

**7** Make waves by rolling out a large rectangle of blue clay. Cut away the top to form the tips of the waves. Blend some darker blue clay into the slab to create depth. Put a piece of clay behind the wave so it will stand up.

# The Set

The set is where you will film your movie. It is the landscape in which your story will come to life. A set can be as simple as a piece of paper taped to the wall or more complex. The set needs to be large enough for your puppets to be able to move around.

## Basic Set

The most basic set is a single piece of paper or poster board. Tape one end of the paper to the wall. Pull the paper and tape the other end to the table. Leave a bit of a curve in the paper.

 *You can build a simple set using a cardboard box. Break down the box and cut out two large rectangles that are the same size.*

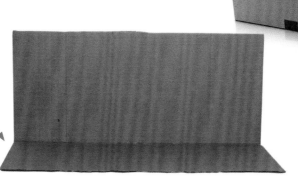

**2** *Line up the long sides of the rectangles and tape them together.*

**3** *Make a triangle from the leftover cardboard.*

**4** *Tape the triangle to the back of the one rectangle. Bend the other to form an L shape as shown.*

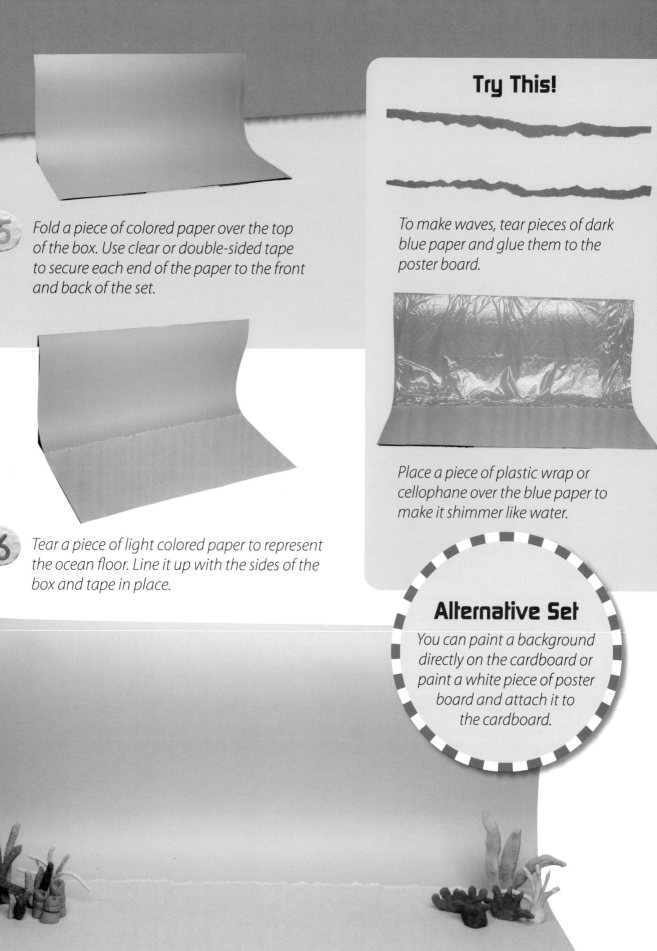

**5** Fold a piece of colored paper over the top of the box. Use clear or double-sided tape to secure each end of the paper to the front and back of the set.

**6** Tear a piece of light colored paper to represent the ocean floor. Line it up with the sides of the box and tape in place.

## Try This!

To make waves, tear pieces of dark blue paper and glue them to the poster board.

Place a piece of plastic wrap or cellophane over the blue paper to make it shimmer like water.

## Alternative Set

You can paint a background directly on the cardboard or paint a white piece of poster board and attach it to the cardboard.

**7** Arrange your props. Before you start shooting, secure the set to the surface you are working on with tape.

# Lights, Camera, . . .

To light your set, a couple of desk lamps or the overhead lights should do the trick. Don't place your set near a window or shoot outside unless it is an overcast day. Changes in lighting will cause flickering in your movie.

*Experiment with the placement of the lamps. Take test shots to see how it looks.*

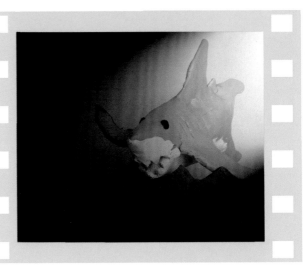

*Flat, even light is created when two lamps are placed an equal distance apart. There are little or no shadows.*

*Make your shark a star! Create a spotlight by directing one light onto the set.*

28

Claymation does not require a video camera. A digital camera, smartphone camera, or tablet camera will work. Think about the camera angles you want to use while shooting your film. The angle and distance from which you capture your scene can bring your movie to life.

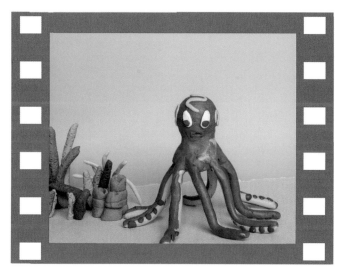

*In a straight-on shot, the camera is lined up directly with the puppet.*

*Shooting the movie from above makes the puppet appear small.*

*A closeup shot taken from a low angle can create a dramatic effect.*

29

# . . . . Action! Making Your Movie

It's time to make your Claymation movie! You have your storyboard, your puppet(s), your set, lights, and camera. Position the puppets on the set when you are ready to begin. Using your storyboard as a guide, start taking photos. Make sure you move your puppets in very tiny increments. The smaller the movements, the smoother the film will be. Be careful not to move the camera while taking a sequence of shots.

*You can use a camera on a tripod, and import your stills later into an animation program. Or you can use your smartphone or tablet camera to capture photos directly in a stop-motion animation app.*

*Make sure your hands are out of the frame after moving the puppet before taking the next shot.*

*It takes a lot of patience to make a Claymation film. Slowly move your puppet toward an object on your set to make it appear as if the puppet is moving on its own. If the puppet moves too far in each shot it will appear to jump rather than move in one fluid motion.*

Now it's time to finish your movie. **Postproduction** is the last step in creating your Claymation film. Within your app or animation program you can edit your frames, removing any that don't work. This is also the time to add music or sound effects. Music can set the mood of the film. Different types of music can sound happy, sad, or suspenseful. There are all kinds of free sound effects on the Internet, or you can record your own. Adding effects to your movie will bring the action to life.

Finally, it's showtime! Stage a screening to share your underwater adventure with an audience. At the end, take a bow!

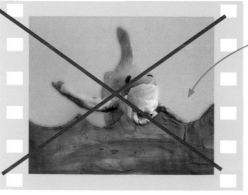

*If there is a scene that doesn't work, cut it!*

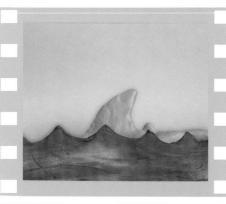

*Use clay letters to make credits for your movie. Include a title and end credits, listing yourself and anyone else who helped.*

# GLOSSARY

**animation** In film, creating the illusion of movement using still images played in a rapid sequence.

**armature** A wire frame that acts as a skeleton for a sculpture made with modeling clay.

**frame** An individual picture in a series of images.

**postproduction** The final stages of finishing a movie after it has been recorded that usually involves editing and adding sound.

**stop-motion** An animation technique that uses a series of shots showing small movements to make characters or objects appear to move.

**storyboard** A series of pictures that show the scenes in an animation.

# FOR MORE INFORMATION

## FURTHER READING

Cassidy, John, and Nicholas Berger. *The Klutz Book of Animation*. Palo Alto, CA: Klutz, 2010.

Cuxart, Bernadette. *Modeling Clay Animals: Easy-to-Follow Projects in Simple Steps*. Hauppauge, NY: Barron's Educational Series, 2010.

Grabham, Tim. *Movie Maker: The Ultimate Guide to Making Films*. Somerville, MA: Candlewick, 2010.

## WEBSITES

For web resources related to the subject of this book, go to: www.windmillbooks.com/weblinks and select this book's title.

# INDEX